PEANUT VS THE PIANO

This hOle book belongs to

_____

Read all the hOle books

PEANUT VS THE PIANO

Yashodhara Lal

Illustrations by Shreya Sen

An imprint of Penguin Random House

DUCKBILL BOOKS

USA | Canada | UK | Ireland | Australia
New Zealand | India | South Africa | China | Singapore

Duckbill Books is part of the Penguin Random House group of companies
whose addresses can be found at global.penguinrandomhouse.com

Published by Penguin Random House India Pvt. Ltd.
4th Floor, Capital Tower 1, MG Road,
Gurugram 122 002, Haryana, India

First published by Duckbill Books 2018
Text copyright © Yashodhara Lal 2018
Illustrations copyright © Shreya Sen 2018

This edition published in Duckbill Books by Penguin Random House India 2020

Yashodhara Lal asserts the moral right to be identified
as the author of this work.

ISBN 9789387103092

Typeset by PrePSol Enterprises Pvt. Ltd.
Printed at Replika Press Pvt. Ltd, India

www.penguin.co.in

This is a legitimate digitally printed version of the book and therefore might not
have certain extra finishing on the cover.

The Monster with Black and White Teeth

'Move over!' Peanut ordered.

The twins, Pickle and Papad, shifted a bit. Peanut plonked herself in the middle of the sofa.

They had just come back from school. Peanut knew very well that they were supposed to do their homework now, but since the twins had switched

 on the TV, she thought she would join in. Just for a bit.

'*Chota Bheem?*' suggested seven-year-old Papad.

'No, no!' Peanut was firm. 'Let's check Netflix—maybe *Full House?*'

'*Full House*, yes!' said Pickle.

Outvoted, Papad flipped around and put his feet up against the back of the sofa. He watched moodily upside down in his favourite sulking position.

Peanut ignored his smelly feet. It was so nice to relax and just watch TV. School wasn't easy in fourth grade.

'What do you guys think you are doing?'

The three kids snapped to attention; Papad scrambling to turn right side up. They looked at Mom with identical sheepish grins.

'Uh, hi, Mom,' said Peanut bravely. 'You're home too early … I mean, you're home early.'

'Yes, I am.' Mom dropped her laptop bag to the floor. She looked cross. 'What have I told you before about doing

your homework before TV on weekdays?'

'I have only ONE homework, Mom,' Pickle said earnestly. 'Maths sheet.'

'And I awso, only ONE homeworks,' piped in Papad. 'English journal.'

'Hmm,' said Mom. 'Well, get to it then.'

Pickle and Papad scrambled off the sofa.

Mom turned to Peanut. 'And you, Peanut?'

'I have three sheets, Mom,' Peanut admitted. 'But I was just going to do them after one—'

'Three!' Mom exclaimed, 'And you have music class in half an hour—what about piano practice?'

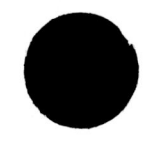

'I didn't practise today, because anyway I'll be playing piano in class.'

'Practice is practice, and class is class,' Mom scolded. 'You have an exam coming up in two months, Moonish Sir has said you must practise forty-five minutes every day.'

The mention of the Grade-3 certification exam made Peanut swallow. 'There isn't enough time,' she protested. 'We come home at four and then have our snack, and then there's homework and …'

'But enough time for TV, eh?' Mom's eye had a dangerous glint and Peanut decided it was better not to argue.

'Go practise.' Mom gestured towards Peanut's shiny dark brown digital piano in the corner of the drawing room. 'We didn't spend so much money on that for nothing.'

Peanut's shoulder slumped. She slid off the sofa and stomped to the piano, switched it on moodily and plonked herself heavily onto the stool.

She began to play her scales. Her fingers ran smoothly over the C major scale, and then D minor, up and down over the black and white keys. But her mind was elsewhere.

It's not fair. Pickle and Papad don't have to practise. Maths and English and Hindi in school, and piano exams too, on top of that.

I hardly have any time. It's just a little TV.

Stupid, boring old piano.

This last thought surprised her and she paused. She had been so excited two years ago when Mom and Dad had bought the piano for her. She had loved her classes when she started. It really had been so much fun. But now …

'Why have you stopped?' Mom's voice snapped Peanut back. 'Hurry, we barely have any time. Play that first song you're going to be tested on? *Spider's Web*, right?'

Peanut sighed and started to play again.

On the way to music school, Peanut gazed unseeingly out of the window.

'What's up, Peanut? Penny for your thoughts,' said Mom.

The trip to the music school was Peanut's only time alone with Mom. She usually told her about what was going on in school and complained about the twins. But today, she just shrugged.

'What are you thinking?' Mom probed.

Peanut had been thinking a few mixed-up thoughts. 'Well, Ma, how come Pickle and Papad don't have to take any music lessons?'

'They will, probably next year when they're old enough,' Mom remarked. 'You know they want to, they've been asking for lessons ever since you started!'

They don't know what they're asking for, Peanut thought, as the car pulled into the driveway of the music school.

Yes, the piano *used* to be fun. Now it was just a big old brown monster.

Monster!!

Monster Moonish Sir

'No-no-no-no-no-no-no!'

Peanut froze, her fingers hovering over the piano keys.

Moonish Sir had a pained expression on his face. His eyes were closed and his lips pursed as if he had been sucking on a sour lemon. His little moustache was all twisted up and though Peanut was a little scared, she couldn't help but think it looked even funnier than usual.

Moonish Sir put his head in his hands for a moment. Then he looked up at her with his big round eyes through his big round spectacles.

'Did I play something … wrong?' Peanut asked.

'No.' Moonish Sir finally spoke. 'You are getting the notes right … but you are only *playing*.'

Peanut wondered what he expected her to do in a piano class. Tap-dance? Or turn somersaults, perhaps? '*Only* playing, sir?'

'Yes,' he said firmly. 'You are playing without any *feeling*.'

'Feeling?' Peanut repeated. 'I don't understand, sir.'

Moonish Sir stood up suddenly. 'Let me show you.'

Peanut vacated her piano stool and Moonish Sir swept majestically into her place. He was a small man but appeared very grand when he sat at the piano. He positioned his unusually long fingers over the piano and peered for a moment at the sheet of music.

The room was suddenly filled with an enchanting melody. Moonish Sir certainly made the same song sound very different. His body swayed back and forth with the music.

She waited for him to finish the

 whole song—the more he played, the less she had to.

The last note rang out long and loud. His eyes were closed and his moustache was vibrating slightly.

Moonish Sir sighed and opened his eyes. His gaze fell on Peanut 'Oh, aha!' he exclaimed, as if just remembering he had a student in the room. 'Well, did you understand?'

Peanut nodded wordlessly.

'There is, young lady,'
Moonish Sir leaned earnestly
towards her, 'a *feeling* to every
piece of music. You understand?'

'I think so, sir.'

'And what is the feeling for this song?'
he urged. 'What are you feeling now?'

Peanut swallowed once. 'Hungry?'

Moonish Sir's moustache drooped.
'Hungry,' he repeated blankly.

'Well, sir,' Peanut hurried to explain,
'usually I have a glass of milk and
biscuits and a little later, some Maggi,
but today Mom said I should practise
and …'

Moonish Sir had his eyes closed
again. 'It's okay, it's okay. Just … play the
way that I was playing, okay?'

'Yes, sir.' Peanut was determined to try.

She sat at the piano and started to play again. But she felt nervous, so it sounded jerky. She remembered how he had been swaying to the music, and started moving back and forth. It didn't feel right, so she decided to sway side-to-side. She rocked her body, but this distracted her and she began to fumble with the notes.

'Stop-stop-stop-stop-stop,' Moonish Sir begged. 'No-no-no-no-no-no-no …'

Peanut stopped.

Moonish Sir bent down so that his head was at the same level as Peanut's. 'Is your stool uncomfortable?'

'No, sir.'

'So why were you jumping around as if you were sitting on a thorny cactus?'

'I was doing what *you* were doing, sir,' Peanut answered earnestly. 'I thought that was the *feeling* you meant?'

Moonish Sir's moustache twisted. He straightened up again and said, 'I will show you once more.'

Peanut obediently got off her seat and he started to play. Once more, the room was filled with the loud, enchanting melody. She stood and watched Moonish Sir's moustache vibrating.

'Well, that was over quick.' Mom stood up as Peanut came out to the reception area.

'Yes.' Peanut glanced over her shoulder. 'Let's go, Mom.'

'What's the hurry?' Mom said, as Peanut tugged at her hand.

Peanut looked back down the long narrow corridor. As she had feared, Moonish Sir was coming.

'Oh, hello, Moonish Sir!' Mom said. 'How nice to see you. I was hoping to ask you how Peanut is coming along.'

Moonish Sir's hair was sticking out in odd places, as if he had been clutching at

it. He glared at Mom. 'How is she coming along?' he repeated.

'Er, well.' Mom looked a little surprised. 'I was hoping *you* would tell me.'

'Madam,' Moonish Sir drew himself up to his full height, 'I am sorry to inform you that if your daughter continues at this pace, she might not be ready for her Grade-3 exam this year.'

'What?' Mom looked aghast. 'But it's just two months away… I thought she was already one out of three songs down?'

'You have said it correctly,' Moonish Sir's moustache twisted to one side. 'She is bringing the song *down*. I am afraid she is losing interest.'

'Losing interest? Of course not.' Mom turned to Peanut. 'You're very interested in the piano, right?'

Peanut appeared to be interested in her shoes. She kicked at the orange carpet, kept her head down and didn't answer.

Mom recovered and said smoothly 'Sir, don't worry. I'll talk to her. It's … it's just been a really long day …'

'Yes,' Moonish Sir wiped his brow. 'It has been a

long day. I must get home. I am developing a headache.'

'Well, yes.' Mom said 'I did mean for *her* but yes, for you too …'

'I must say, Missus Madam,' Moonish Sir interrupted her, 'she will have to work harder. If it takes this long to cover each song, she will miss the examination date. So we must focus! Increase practice time to one hour at home now!'

'All right,' Mom agreed.

Peanut looked up in panic from Moonish Sir's stern face to Mom's determined one. Her shoulders slumped. She kicked at the orange carpet, a little more savagely this time.

Monster Aunty

'Hey, where're you going?' Peanut twisted around on her piano stool.

Pickle and Papad were heading for the door, holding large plastic bowls in their hands.

'We're gonna feed the doggies,' announced Papad.

'No, you're not,' Peanut snapped. 'Mom said we can only do that on Saturdays.'

'I *awready* called Mom,' said Pickle. 'I tolded her that Shera was looking hungry and maybe no one fed them today.'

'Are you coming?' Papad asked Peanut.

'I have to practise.' Peanut said glumly. 'For an hour!'

'An hour!' Papad exclaimed. 'A full tharty minutes?'

'Never mind.' Peanut rolled her eyes.

She was tempted to go with Pickle and Papad. It would only take a few minutes. She sprang up, slammed the piano-lid shut and skipped along after the twins. 'Wait for me, guys!'

It was a beautiful day. Peanut had a skip in her step, she was so happy to be outside and free. She liked nothing

better than hanging out with the four colony pups—Shera, Shannon, Binny and Bobby.

The pups weren't really pups anymore. They were almost a year old, and had grown really big. Shera, the biggest and the naughtiest of them all, let out a bark when he saw the children approaching the dog shelter, and all four dogs ran up, tails wagging.

Pickle and Papad used to be afraid
of dogs but not any more. Dark brown
Shannon was Pickle's favourite, and
Papad couldn't decide between the black
twins Binny and Bobby. Peanut liked
Shera best—maybe because Shera, like
her, was the oldest, and also somehow
always getting into trouble.

The guards near the gate watched
warily as the children fed the dogs.
Some of them didn't like the dogs.

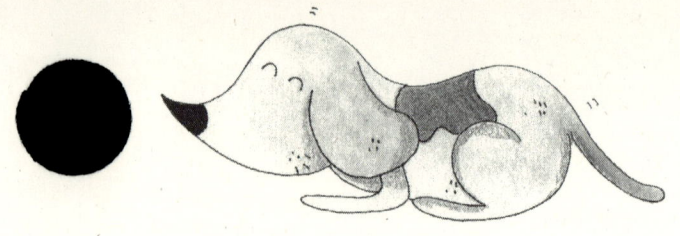

'How silly, to allow mongrels in here like this!' came a loud rasping voice.

Two unfamiliar men in brown uniforms were at the gate. One was short and plump, the other tall and skinny, but both had nasty, sour expressions on their faces. Shera looked up from his milk-mush bowl and growled at them.

'Your names,' said the guard to the men, indicating his register. 'Enter them here.'

'Can't read or write,' said the short one in his rasping voice. 'We're here for a gardening job. You write. I'm Ram

Prasad and this is Lakshman Prasad.'

'Where is this Jain Madam's house?' the tall man asked the guard.

Peanut grimaced. Jain Aunty lived right opposite their place. She was a sour, grumpy woman, who lived alone and was always complaining. She hated the dogs and often scolded the children for feeding them. Well, at least she'd put these two new gardeners in their place.

The gardeners went off in the direction that the guard pointed. Peanut stroked Shera's back absently. He finished and then tried to lick her hand. She sighed. 'I gotta go back and practise.'

'We'll stay here,' said Pickle.

'Mom said no wandering about alone.'

'We're not alone,' said Papad. 'I'm with Pickle.'

'And I'm with Papad,' piped in Pickle.

Peanut glared at them, gave each of the dogs a last quick pat and walked away.

The two gardeners were peering at bushes right outside Mrs Jain's building, opposite Peanut's home. She hurried past them and ran into the house.

'Not fair. One hour!' Peanut mumbled as she plonked herself on the stool and snapped open the lid to reveal the piano's black and white teeth. She stared unseeingly at her music. *Spider's Web*. She felt like she was stuck *in* a spider's web.

She played a few notes but they sounded weak and soft to her. She cranked up the volume on her piano and played the notes again. They rang out loud, and in the silence of the house, the notes startled her. She set her jaw and angrily turned up the piano volume to full—she'd never tried it that loud before. She banged both hands down on the keys.

JHHHHHHHAAAAAAANNNNNNNNGGGGGG.

aaaah!

JHHHHHHHAAAAAAANNNNNNNGGGG

'Peanut!' Kajal Didi protested. 'Why are you playing so loudly?'

Peanut drowned out the sound of Kajal Didi's protests by smashing both hands down again. It was very satisfying.

Peanut ran her hands wildly over the piano from left to right, starting with the low C and ending on the high E. It had a loud squealy, screechy quality to it—**EEEEEEEEE**. As she let it fade, she heard an '**OWWWWWWWW**' from outside in the exact same pitch.

'Stop it, Pickle-Papad.' Peanut called. She could hear her brothers giggling outside.

'It's not us!' came Papad's excited voice. 'It's Shera, Peanut Didi! He came

 running here—he likes that note, play it again?'

'What?' Peanut went to the window.

Shera was on both hind-legs, his howl just fading. She'd never seen him do that. She ran back to the piano and played a few different notes loudly again.

'No, play that *really* high note again,' called Pickle from outside.

Peanut jammed her finger down on the high E again. **EEEEEEEEEE** ...

'**OWWWWWWWWWW** …'
came the howling sound from outside.

Peanut grinned as she heard her brothers giggling. 'Again, again!' they urged.

'Peanut, stop it!' said Kajal Didi, her voice adding to the cacophony. 'Stop it! Stop it! Be QUIEEEEET!'

EEEEEEEE …

rang out under Peanut's stubborn finger.

'**OWWWWWWWW** …'

The sound of her brothers' giggles from outside caused Peanut to double up in laughter herself.

'WHAT'S GOING ON HERE? STOP IT IMMEDIATELY, ALL OF YOU.'

OWWWWwwww ...'

Peanut froze. Pickle-Papad's laughter stopped. Shera's howl turned into a small whimper and then died away.

Peanut swallowed as she went to the balcony. It was a voice way scarier than even Mum's.

It was the voice of Jain Aunty.

Miss Monster Peanut

'Mom made your practice one-and-a-half hours?' Pickle whispered that night, as the three kids lay in bed. It was dark but none of them were sleepy.

Peanut ignored him. She sniffled and turned away to face the wall.

'One inda haff hours?' Papad exclaimed. 'A full FORTY-FIVE minutes!'

'Oh shut up, Papad,' said Peanut

grumpily. 'Learn how to tell time first.'

'Quiet!' came Mum's voice from outside. 'All of you.'

'She's mad at *all* of us bicoz of you, Peanut Didi,' said Papad resentfully.

'Me!' Peanut sat up in bed. 'You're the ones who said do eeeeeeee ...'

'Peanut!' came Mom's voice.

Pickle whispered, 'That naughty Jain Aunty, she wuz the one who complained to Mom ...'

Even though Peanut had apologised, Mrs Jain had called Mom up. Mom and Mrs Jain didn't really like each other, and Mom had not liked having to apologise to her.

'Your piano is not a toy,' Mom had scolded Peanut in the evening. 'You don't seem to understand you're supposed to take your exams seriously.' And she had decided that Peanut needed to put in even *more* practice time.

'Well, we'll see about the exams.' Peanut whispered into the dark now, more to herself than her brothers. Something Moonish Sir had said had given her an idea. 'I know how to handle them.'

'Whatcha gonna do?' Pickle asked curiously.

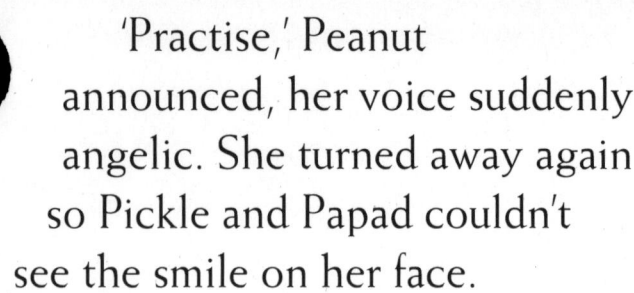 'Practise,' Peanut announced, her voice suddenly angelic. She turned away again so Pickle and Papad couldn't see the smile on her face.

'No-no-no-no-no-no!' Moonish Sir looked heavenward as if for some relief. Peanut tried not to giggle.

'I'm sorry, Moonish Sir. I don't know why I keep getting it wrong.'

'But you almost *had* this song!' Moonish Sir said despairingly. 'It was just the finishing touches, the final feeling that was needed ...'

'Yes, sir,' Peanut said innocently. 'I'm just not able to get the notes.'

'Have you been practising this week?'

'Oh, yes, sir,' Peanut replied

immediately. 'You can ask my mom; I've been doing one-and-a-half hours.' She sighed. 'Maybe it's too much practice?'

'Hummph!' snorted Moonish Sir disbelievingly. 'Well, try it again.'

'I doubt she will be ready for her exam, Madam,' Moonish Sir announced to

Mom. 'She is obviously not practising enough.'

'But, sir, no, she has!' said Mom. 'She's been quite good about it over the last few days. Her practice time has increased.'

'Have you heard her play, Madam?'

'I'm not there through every practice session,' Mom said. 'But I *have* heard her play that spider song repeatedly. I thought it was coming along quite well, actually.'

'Well,' said Moonish Sir, sniffing in a snotty manner. 'Perhaps it is "quite well" to you, Madam. But I, as the *teacher*, can assure you that she is not ready. If she can't even do that one, how are we to prepare her for the other two?'

Mom said icily, 'Well, I'll have you know that I have been a student of music myself. I think she *is* indeed ready for Grade-3 exams. Perhaps there is something wrong with the way you are assessing her.'

Moonish Sir drew himself up to his full height again. 'You insult me, Madam! There is nothing wrong with my assessment. If a child isn't ready for the next level, she isn't ready. No point in wasting time.'

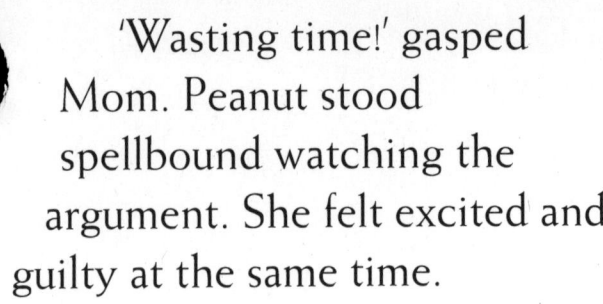 'Wasting time!' gasped Mom. Peanut stood spellbound watching the argument. She felt excited and guilty at the same time.

'I don't understand.' Peanut strained to hear her mom's voice through the door. 'How can he say she isn't ready? Just a couple of months back, Moonish was sure she would sail through. I think she's doing just fine but …'

'Whatcha doin?' Papad's voice right behind her made Peanut jump.

'Shhh. I'm trying to hear what Mom is saying.'

'Just open da door,' Papad suggested.

Peanut shushed him again, so he shrugged and put his ear to the door, like her.

Peanut strained to listen. Suddenly, the door opened and they both lost their balance and fell in a heap on the floor.

'What are you two doing?' Mom demanded. Not waiting for an answer, she turned to Peanut. 'Peanut, you practised today?'

'Oh yes, Mom.' Peanut said. 'You can ask Kajal Didi. Or Pickle-Papad. I played for a really long time even before class.'

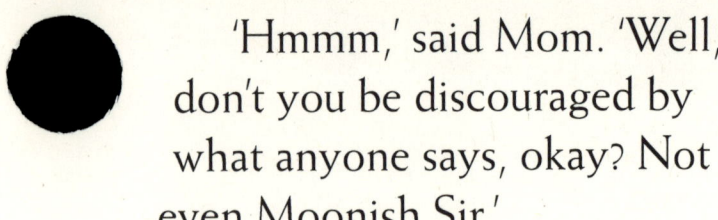'Hmmm,' said Mom. 'Well, don't you be discouraged by what anyone says, okay? Not even Moonish Sir.'

'Thanks, Mom,' said Peanut sweetly. 'I'll just keep trying my best. Can I go read my book now, Mom?'

'Go ahead,' Mom sighed. 'As long as your homework and practice are all done.'

'All done,' sang out Peanut and she ran to the sofa. Soon she was lost in her story.

So lost, that she didn't notice that Papad was trotting towards her piano. So lost, that she didn't see him sit down at it, open up the lid, and switch on the button as he had seen her do so many times. So lost, that she didn't see him press the button on the left; the one that played the recordings of what she had played earlier.

The melody of *Spider's Web* rang out through the house.

'Papad, stop that! Stop it!'

Peanut sprang up and rushed to the piano to switch it off. But it was too late.

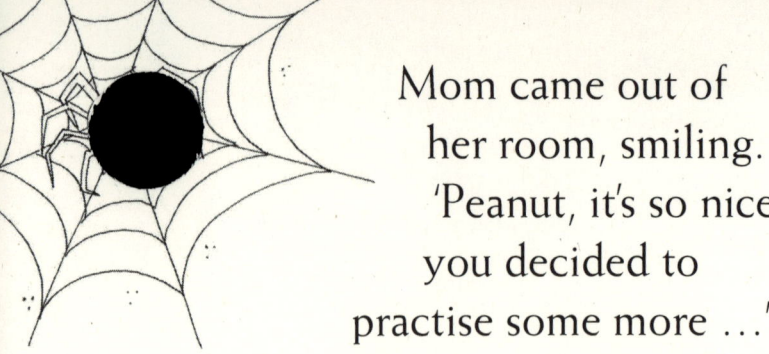

Mom came out of
her room, smiling.
'Peanut, it's so nice
you decided to
practise some more ...'

Her voice trailed off as
she saw that it was Papad sitting on the
piano stool, his little fingers banging
away at the keys, eyes closed as he
pretended to play *Spider's Web*.

She looked from Papad to Peanut's
guilty face—and Mum knew exactly
what had been going on.

Goodbye, Monster Piano

'So, no more piano exams?' Srishti's voice came floating over the phone.

'Yeah,' Peanut twisted the wire of the landline around her finger distractedly. 'Mom says since I don't like the piano anymore, she'll pull me out of lessons.'

'Okay,' Srishti exclaimed. 'But why don't you sound happy then?'

'Happy?' Peanut bit her lip. 'I am happy, of course. It's just that … Mom said she's also going to *sell* the piano.'

'But you said the piano was like a monster!'

'Yeah.' Peanut said glumly. 'A real monster.' She cleared her throat and said in a brighter voice. 'So listen, since I'm free this weekend, you wanna ask your mom if maybe you can come over?'

'No chance!' Srishti's voice was glum, 'I have gymnastics practice—and tomorrow there's a tournament.'

'Umm, okay. Maybe I'll check with Aanya for this weekend.'

'Aanya's got art class,' Srishti said immediately. 'She's moving to a more advanced level now. And Sammaira has dance practice.' She sighed. 'I guess you're the only one with a lot of free time. So lucky!'

'Free time,' Peanut repeated. 'I guess I am lucky.'

Peanut decided she would go look for Pickle and Papad who were somewhere in the park. Mom and Dad were out shopping.

Peanut was a little surprised that Mom hadn't yelled at her—but she had seemed more disappointed than angry.

'If you hated the piano that much, you should have just told me,' she'd said.

Peanut had just looked down at the ground sullenly. She felt a little ashamed of what she had done but didn't want to admit it. After all, it *was* unfair. One-and-a-half hours of practice every day!

Pickle and Papad were in the small park near their house, playing cricket. Ah, well. She didn't like cricket. She went off to look for the dogs.

But the dogs weren't near the shelter. 'Shera,' Peanut called, hopefully. 'Shera, where are you?'

'Looking for that silly brown mutt?' The rasping voice behind her made her jump. 'The dog-catchers must have got him.'

It was Ram Prasad and Laxman Prasad. Ram Prasad had a crooked grin on his face. 'No-good creatures. Nuisances, all of them. Good they've gone.'

'They've not gone anywhere,' Peanut said more confidently than she felt. 'It's just not feeding time. They must be somewhere around.'

'Well, if they come near us when we're working, we'll give them a good kick,' said Ram Prasad, and the other man nodded.

Peanut glowered at them, and turned on her heel and walked away. This walk wasn't turning out to be very nice.

She would go home and read. But she didn't feel like going inside the house. Seeing the piano in the drawing room made her a little sad.

She remembered the day she had got it. Her parents had set it up as a surprise for her while she had been out playing. Mom had covered Peanut's eyes as she guided her into the house. Peanut had reached out and felt the cool wooden lid and squealed in delight and hugged her parents.

'So, young lady,' Mrs Jain's loud voice stopped Peanut in her tracks. The old lady always walked up and down in front of her own building. 'I hear you are getting rid of that noisy instrument of yours. Good riddance, I say!'

'How-how did you know, Aunty?' stammered Peanut.

'I know everything!' said Mrs Jain grandly. 'And also, your mother put it up on the noticeboards in all the buildings.

 If I had the money, I'd buy it myself and send it all the way to Timbuktoo.'

Mrs Jain looked beyond her and snapped. 'Ah, there you are. Good-for-nothing gardeners. When are you going to finish trimming these bushes?'

Ram Prasad and Laxman Prasad walked up. 'Arrey, Jain Madamji,' Ram Prasad said. 'We had done them yesterday—those silly dogs must have messed them up.'

Peanut escaped into her house.

Much later that night, long after Pickle and Papad and even her parents and Kajal Didi were asleep, Peanut found herself wide awake, tossing and turning in bed.

She wouldn't ever get to go to the music school again.

Moonish Sir wasn't so bad. He had taught her a lot and he played really beautifully himself. She had enjoyed it when he played, and not just because of the way his moustache quivered. She had wished she could play like him one day.

Well, that wasn't ever going to happen. Mom said Ranaditya's mother was coming in tomorrow to look at her piano. She realised sadly, the piano wasn't going to be *hers* anymore. Mom had told her she shouldn't touch it now that it was going to be sold.

She sighed and stared up at the ceiling. To not be allowed to touch it. That old monster. That old beautiful monster. On which she had learned to

 play so many songs, starting right from *Twinkle Twinkle Little Star*. So many songs …

She sat up. She sneaked out of bed, careful not to wake Pickle and Papad. She stole past Kajal Didi, sleeping on the charpoy in the corner. She walked stealthily past her parents' bedroom.

Mom had said not to touch the piano—but she just felt she had to, one final time.

She found her way to it easily despite the darkness. She ran her hands over the cool wood, marvelling at the smoothness. Three years. And she was going to lose it tomorrow.

A tear formed in the corner of her left eye, and she blinked it away quickly.

As she turned to go back, she heard a whisper. She stole closer to the balcony door, which was half-open. Who could it be at this time?

'Been three hours. The old lady must be asleep.'

'Now,' replied a rasping voice. What were Ram Prasad and his crony up to?

Peanut slipped through the half-open door and looked through the balcony netting. They were crouching right under it.

Oh no! It looked like they were planning to break into Mrs Jain's house! Peanut had always felt there was something suspicious about the two. Shera had growled at them. Poor Mrs Jain who lived alone and was so old …

The two men crept across the road and headed to Mrs Jain's window.

Peanut's mind was racing as fast as her heart. She had to go and wake

up her parents right away.
What if it took too long to
explain things? She had to
do something fast to raise an
alarm—but what?

Peanut rushed back into the
drawing room. She flipped open the
piano lid in one smooth motion,
switched it on, turned up the volume
to full and jammed both hands down as
hard as she could.

JHHHHHHHAAAAAAANNNNNNNGGGGGG ...

The clanging sound rang through
the house and through the colony,
shattering the silence of the night.
Peanut lifted her fingers high again.

JHHHHHHHHHHHHAAAAAAANNNGGGG ...

'Oh baba goh!' Kajal Didi shrieked.
'What is it, who is it?'

'Peanut?' Mom switched on the light and stared disbelievingly. 'What on earth are you doing? Have you lost your marbles?'

'Mom!' Peanut yelled. 'It's a robbery! Call the police!!'

'The police!' Mom yelled. 'I'll call the mental asylum. What's wrong with you? Stop immediately!'

'No Mom, you don't understand. Dad, Dad!'

There wasn't a moment to lose. Peanut turned back to the piano

JJHHHHHHAAANNNNGGGG.

'WHAT IS THAT INFERNAL NOISE?'

Peanut could have wept for joy as she heard Mrs Jain's voice yelling from the next building. At least, the old lady was safe. But those two nasty gardeners were going to get away with it. Unless …

'It's alright, Mrs Jain, just a little misunderstanding … taking care of it!' Mom called from the balcony. She grabbed hold of Peanut's arm and pulled her away. Peanut jerked her arm free.

 Pickle and Papad and Dad were all in the drawing room, and there was complete chaos.

Mum was still trying to restrain her, but with one final superhuman effort, Peanut hit the exact note she was looking for.

EEEEEEEEEEEEEEEEEE ...

The high E rang out and Pickle-Papad covered their ears with their hands. Peanut pressed down determinedly.

'**OWWWWWWWWWWW** ...'
came the answering howl from outside.

'What's going on?' Dad shouted.

The howling changed to a ferocious growl. There were men shouting, including one rasping 'Get away, you stupid mongrel. There, take that!' Then a loud yell.

Papad clapped his hands in glee in the balcony. 'Mom! Shera bit nasty man in the bottom!'

Mom peered out of the window and gasped. 'What are those two men doing out there?'

Peanut ran to the balcony. Shera had his teeth deep into the leg of Lakshman Prasad, who hopped around trying to get free. Ram Prasad was clutching his bottom.

'The guards are on their way.' Dad was on the phone. 'These men must have planned to …'

'Rob Mrs Jain's house!' Peanut finished breathlessly. 'I heard them!'

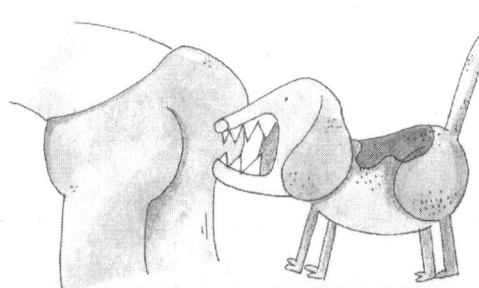

'YOU NAUGHTY LITTLE GIRL AND YOUR STUPID DOGS!' Mrs Jain's voice came ringing out. 'WAKING UP THE WHOLE NEIGHBORHOOD! SUCH NONSENSE!'

The guards hauled off the two robbers and Shera disappeared into the night.

Peanut leaned back, weak with relief, not even caring that Mrs Jain was angry. What mattered was that the old lady was safe.

She looked up and found Mom looking at her with a puzzled frown.

'What were you doing up in the middle of the night, though, Peanut?'

So Peanut told her.

The next week, Peanut was back at her piano lessons. She was going to miss her exams but she was okay with that. To her surprise, so was Mom. Moonish Sir beamed at her as she played *Spider's Web* perfectly and with *feeling*.

And these days, when she sat at her piano, it didn't seem like a monster any more.

Yashodhara Lal makes people laugh (with her best-selling romantic-comedy books), makes them sweat (with her high-energy Zumba classes) and sometimes makes them sweat harder (as boss-lady in the corporate world!). Know more about her, her family and writing on www.yashodharalal.com.

Shreya Sen's earliest memories are of her mom dragging her to book fairs, in Assam. Her favourite pastime was to gorge on Russian picture books and draw on the walls. This led to her studying animation film design at NID, Ahmedabad. A summer internship at a children's publication house made her believe that this is what she wants to do for the rest of her life. She believes that one draws with the mind, and not the hand. Her favourite artist is Henry Matisse.

Read more adventures of Peanut

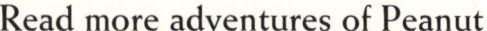

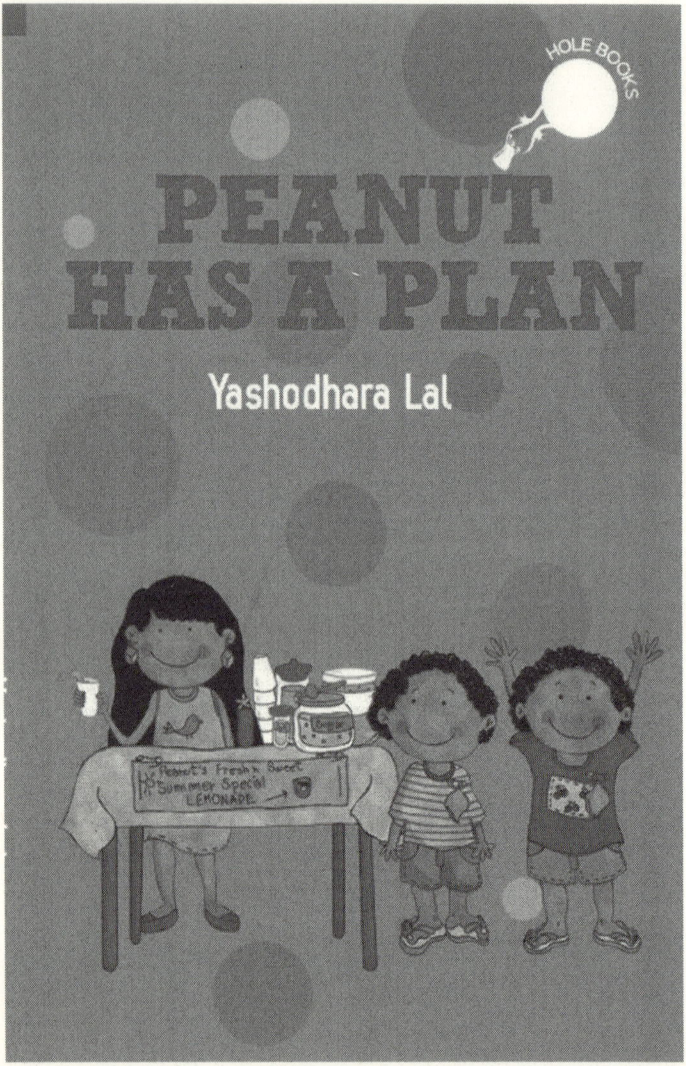